CW01082837

Original title:

Nourishing Friendships

Author: Aron Pilviste

ISBN HARDBACK: 978-9916-89-109-4

ISBN PAPERBACK: 978-9916-89-110-0

ISBN EBOOK: 978-9916-89-111-7

The Light of Companionship

In shadows deep where silence sighs,
Two souls entwined beneath the skies.
Their laughter dances, sweet and bright,
A beacon glows, a guiding light.

Through storms that rage and winds that howl,
Together they stand, a sturdy prow.
With every tear and every smile,
They walk hand in hand, mile after mile.

When doubts arise and dreams feel lost,
They share the warmth, no matter the cost.
In whispered hopes and gentle care,
They weave their love, a bond so rare.

In quiet moments, hearts align,
In every glance, a spark divine.
With memories made and stories told,
Their journey thrives, a treasure of gold.

As time marches on and days unfold,
Their light grows stronger, stories told.
In each other's arms, they find their way,
The light of companionship, come what may.

Laughter in the Autumn Air

Leaves dance like laughter, soft and bright,
Children play with joy, hearts take flight.
Chilly breezes carry cheerful sounds,
In this crisp season, happiness abounds.

Pumpkins gleam in twilight's embrace,
Families gather, smiles on each face.
The crunch of leaves beneath small feet,
Echoes of laughter, a melody sweet.

Echoes of Shared Secrets

In quiet corners, whispers flow,
Secrets linger, as friendships grow.
A glance, a smile, a knowing nod,
In the heart's garden, memories trod.

Moonlight weaves through the gentle night,
Promises shared, holding them tight.
In the silence, trust takes its place,
Each echo a bond, each moment a trace.

Threads of Golden Light

Sunrise spills gold on the waking ground,
Each ray a promise, softly profound.
Nature whispers, as life starts anew,
Golden threads weaving the morning's hue.

Time dances in shadows, light intertwines,
A tapestry formed, where the heart aligns.
With every sigh, the day begins,
New adventures await, where joy springs.

Invitations to the Hearth

In cozy corners, warmth envelops all,
Firelight flickers, casting a call.
Friends gather close, sharing their tales,
With laughter and love, the spirit prevails.

Hot cocoa swirls in the gentle night,
Stories unfold in the dancing light.
Each heart a flame, bright and sincere,
Invitations to the hearth, where all draw near.

Roots of Compassion

In silence we nurture, the seeds of care,
A touch, a smile, shared moments rare.
Through storms and shadows, we gently grow,
Bound by the love we choose to sow.

Hands held together, strong and true,
In the garden of hearts, where kindness blooms anew.
We stand united, through joy and pain,
The roots of compassion, our eternal gain.

Echoes of Understanding

In whispered thoughts, we find our way,
The echoes of trust, in what we say.
With every heartbeat, a promise to share,
In the bond of understanding, we're always there.

Moments of silence, where hearts align,
The dance of empathy, gentle and fine.
Through laughter and tears, together we stand,
In the shadows of doubt, we reach for each hand.

Harvesting Moments

Under the sun, where the wildflowers grow,
We gather the moments, in a soft golden glow.
With every heartbeat, we pause and reflect,
In the tapestry woven, our treasures connect.

The simple joys, in the laughter we share,
Are the sweetest of memories, beyond compare.
In the fields of time, our hearts intertwine,
Harvesting moments, both yours and mine.

The Ties that Bind

In the fabric of life, we weave and mend,
Threads of connection, around every bend.
Through struggles and triumphs, we rise and fall,
These ties that bind us, we cherish them all.

With love as our guide, we journey the way,
In the warmth of each heartbeat, we find our stay.
A circle of friendship, a bond that won't break,
In every shared heartbeat, our stories awake.

The Embrace of Time

In the hush of twilight's glow,
Moments dance, they ebb and flow.
Shadows sway with whispers soft,
Memories linger, dreams take off.

Time's embrace, a gentle sigh,
Holding secrets as they fly.
In its arms, we learn to wait,
Unraveling life's woven fate.

Hours pass, yet still we stand,
Within the grasp of fate's own hand.
Elusive, yet so bold and bright,
Time's embrace, our guiding light.

Petals in Full Bloom

In gardens where the colors play,
Petals stretch beneath the day.
Softly fragrant, vibrant hues,
Nature's canvas, endless views.

Bees hum softly, skies of blue,
Every bloom a story true.
In the sun, they dance and sway,
Whispers of the bright bouquet.

Morning dew like diamonds cling,
To the petals, life takes wing.
In full bloom, they proudly share,
Beauty found everywhere.

Mornings Brewed with Laughter

Sunlight spills through open blinds,
A symphony of coffee finds.
Laughter dances in the air,
Joyful moments we all share.

Chirping birds and sizzling pans,
Waking dreams, we make our plans.
Each sip warms the chilled morning,
With each giggle, heart is soaring.

Stories brewed like fragrant beans,
In the warmth, friendship gleans.
Mornings shine with laughter's grace,
In this haven, life we chase.

Bridges Built on Kindness

Through the valleys, strong and wide,
Bridges span with arms open wide.
Crafted from compassion's heart,
In kindness, we play our part.

Every step, a gentle bridge,
Building pathways, breaking ridge.
Hands together, hearts unite,
In the dark, we shine so bright.

Words like bricks we place with care,
Crafting futures, dreams to share.
Upon these bridges, we shall find,
That love and kindness are combined.

The Dance of Trust

In shadows soft, our hearts align,
Each whispered word, a fragile sign.
We take a step, then spin around,
In this embrace, pure love is found.

Through every doubt, we rise and sway,
Each secret shared, a brighter day.
With gentle grace, we move as one,
Trust leads us forth, our fears outrun.

In rhythm slow, we learn to bend,
A dance of souls, where time can mend.
Our laughter rings, a sweet refrain,
In this ballet, we break the chain.

With every turn, we lose the past,
A melody that holds us fast.
The world may fade, but here we gleam,
In perfect time, we find our dream.

The music fades, but hearts still beat,
Upon this stage, we find our seat.
In silence deep, our spirits soar,
In trust's embrace, we are evermore.

A Cup Overflowing

With every sip, a story shared,
In porcelain warmth, our souls laid bare.
The steam rises, a sweet perfume,
In this simple cup, love finds room.

Memories swirl like cream above,
Each drop a token, a cup of love.
Laughter lingers, like honeyed tea,
In every taste, you are with me.

The world outside may rush and race,
But here we pause, in time's embrace.
The clink of cups, a toast to years,
In every drink, we drown our fears.

Warmth of friendship fills the air,
As confidences float, light as air.
In every pour, our hopes ignite,
A cup overflowing, pure delight.

So let us brew, and let us share,
In this small moment, we lay bare.
With every cup, our spirits soar,
In this joy, we find much more.

Stars in Each Other's Eyes

On starlit nights, we intertwine,
Your gaze a universe, so divine.
In every glance, a story told,
With every spark, our hearts unfold.

We weave a tapestry of light,
In every blink, the world feels right.
Your laughter echoes in the air,
Stars in each other's eyes, we stare.

As constellations dance above,
We find our paths, a tale of love.
In whispered dreams, we lose the space,
A galaxy found in each embrace.

With every heartbeat, time stands still,
In cosmic wonder, we bend our will.
Your light, my guide, through endless skies,
In twilight's glow, our spirits rise.

Forever lost, in this vast sea,
Of stars that twinkle endlessly.
With every wish, we find our place,
Stars in each other's eyes, a grace.

Symphonies of the Everyday

In morning light, the kettle sings,
A gentle hum, the day it brings.
With every stir, a rhythm flows,
In simple tasks, the beauty grows.

The rustling leaves, a whispered tune,
Beneath the sun, beneath the moon.
In every laugh, in every sigh,
A symphony of days gone by.

The clatter of dishes, a song we know,
In shared routines, our spirits flow.
Each heartbeat shared, a note so clear,
In harmony, we conquer fear.

The rain's soft patter, a soothing beat,
In puddles jumping, our joy's repeat.
Through trials faced, together we rise,
In life's great score, love never lies.

So let us dance through ordinary,
In all that's small, find legendary.
For in each moment, life displays,
A symphony of our tender days.

The Language of Understanding

In silence we speak, hearts intertwined,
Words unneeded, our souls aligned.
A glance, a nod, the warmth we share,
A bond unbroken, beyond compare.

Through whispers soft, we find our way,
Navigating the night and day.
In gestures kind, truths revealed,
A language of love, forever sealed.

In laughter bright, or sorrow's shade,
Together we stand, unafraid.
The world fades away, just us two,
In the language of understanding, so true.

With every touch, every sigh,
We build our world, just you and I.
No need for words, our hearts will speak,
In the quiet moments, it's you I seek.

Through life's trials, side by side,
In this sacred space, we'll abide.
For love is a journey, not just a start,
Connected forever, in heart to heart.

Seasons of Unspoken Care

In spring's bloom, the world awakes,
Gentle breezes, as the earth shakes.
A tender touch, a soft embrace,
In every season, love finds its place.

Summer's glow, with laughter near,
Days so long, and hearts held dear.
Silences linger, as joy cascades,
In moments shared, our love invades.

Autumn leaves fall, colors collide,
With every hue, I know you're beside.
The chill in the air, yet warmth in sight,
A quiet comfort, through day and night.

Winter's grasp, with snowflakes rare,
In the stillness, we're aware.
The hearth is warm, our spirits blend,
In every heartbeat, love does transcend.

Through each season, our bond remains,
In unspoken care, love sustains.
A journey of life in every layer,
Time keeps us wrapped in sweet prayer.

A Quilt of Memories

Each patch a story, stitched with care,
Moments woven, the joy we share.
In colors bright, and shadows deep,
A quilt of memories, ours to keep.

Laughter echoes in every thread,
Tales of love, both spoken and read.
With every stitch, life's fabric grows,
In the warmth of memory, my heart knows.

From whispered dreams to battles fought,
In this quilt, each lesson taught.
Through every tear and joy we glean,
A tapestry rich, in every scene.

As years entwine, new patches shine,
Creating a life, uniquely divine.
In every fold, a truth revealed,
A quilt of memories, lovingly sealed.

So rest your head, beneath this art,
A sheltering embrace, from the start.
In the softness of love, we shall lie,
Together forever, you and I.

Walking Side by Side

Through winding paths and open skies,
We tread together, you and I.
With every step, the world unfolds,
In quiet moments, our story told.

In shadows cast, or sun's bright glare,
Life's journey shared, knowing we care.
With hands entwined, hearts beat as one,
In every trial, together we run.

The hills may rise, the valleys dip,
Yet side by side, we'll never slip.
In laughter light, or tears that fall,
Together we conquer, together we crawl.

Through every dawn, and dusk's embrace,
In this dance of life, we find our place.
With every mile, love grows more wide,
In this sweet journey, walking side by side.

No need for words, our steps align,
In every silence, our hearts combine.
For as we walk this path so free,
Forever, you walk along with me.

Echoing Support

In shadows deep, a voice rings clear,
A gentle whisper, soothing fear.
With every heartbeat, strength we find,
Together, always, intertwined.

Through stormy nights and endless days,
We lift each other in countless ways.
With hands held tight, we stand as one,
In this journey, our battles won.

The echoes bounce, they carry far,
A promise kept, our guiding star.
In laughter shared and tears set free,
Support flows boundless, like the sea.

So when the path grows dim and frail,
Remember well, we will not fail.
In unity, we face the test,
Together we soar, forever blessed.

Memories Under the Moon

Beneath the silver moonlit glow,
We dance with shadows, soft and slow.
Whispers of times, both lost and found,
In memories, our hearts are wound.

Each twinkling star, a story shared,
Of laughter, dreams, and moments dared.
With each heartbeat, memories replay,
Under the moon, we'll find our way.

The gentle breeze recalls the past,
In fleeting moments, hopes are cast.
With every sigh, the night unfolds,
Our secrets whispered, softly told.

In vivid hues, the night inspires,
Igniting deep, forgotten fires.
Together, in this sacred space,
We find our peace, sweet moonlit grace.

A Sanctuary of Trust

In quiet corners, truth resounds,
A safe embrace where peace abounds.
In whispered thoughts, we lay our fears,
An open heart, through all the years.

With every secret, bonds grow tight,
In this haven, we find our light.
Through trials faced and joys we share,
A sanctuary, always there.

With kindness woven into our walls,
Love echoes soft when darkness calls.
In trust, we rise, we stand our ground,
In unity, our strength is found.

So here we gather, side by side,
In this refuge, there's naught to hide.
Through every storm, we'll brave the tide,
A sanctuary where we abide.

Blossoming Insight

In gardens vast, where thoughts take flight,
Seeds of wisdom bloom in light.
With gentle hands, we tend and nurture,
Transforming dreams with every suture.

Through trials faced, we come to grow,
In moments still, true colors show.
Each lesson learned, a petal wide,
From hardships faced, our truths collide.

The beauty found in struggle's pain,
Emerging strength like springtime rain.
With every dawn, new paths emerge,
A blossoming, a quiet surge.

In minds that wander and hearts set free,
We find our way, we learn to see.
In every thought, insight ignites,
A tapestry of endless lights.

A Tapestry of Comfort

In the warmth of a gentle embrace,
Threads of companionship intertwine,
Soft whispers of solace in space,
Creating a haven, pure and divine.

A radiant light through the fabric shines,
Colors of laughter, woven with care,
The patterns tell stories, the heart aligns,
In this sanctuary, burdens are rare.

Moments like jewels, precious and bright,
Adorned with the love that we hold dear,
Stitched in a tapestry, joy takes flight,
Comfort found here, free from all fear.

With every thread, our spirits entwined,
A gentle reminder, we're never apart,
Peace in the quiet, connection aligned,
A tapestry woven from heart to heart.

The Sweetness of Connection

Two souls collide in a cosmic dance,
Whispers of laughter in the night air,
In shared moments, we find romance,
A sweetness that lingers everywhere.

Hands clasped together, a bond so tight,
Eyes sparkling bright under a starlit gaze,
With every heartbeat, we take flight,
In this connection, our spirits blaze.

Time slows down as we cherish the now,
Each second echoes with vibrant delight,
Weaving our dreams into fate's soft vow,
The sweetness of union feels just right.

With kindness and love, we build a bridge,
Linking our worlds with threads of gold,
In this embrace, we honor the edge,
Of all that was, and all that will unfold.

Where Shadows Meet the Light

In twilight's hush, the magic begins,
A dance of shadows, soft and low,
Where dreams take flight and hope spins,
In the gentle glow, we find our flow.

The sun dips low, painting hues so bright,
As shadows whisper tales of the past,
In the embrace of day turning night,
We gather courage, our hopes steadfast.

Each flicker of light reveals a way,
Guiding us through the uncertain dark,
In the heart of night, we boldly sway,
Trusting our paths, igniting a spark.

Where shadows gather, love remains clear,
A journey unfolds in the soft twilight,
In the space between, we conquer fear,
Where shadows meet, we ignite the light.

Moments that Savor

A taste of joy in every bite,
The sweetness lingers on the tongue,
In moments savored, pure delight,
Where time stands still, and love is sung.

Laughter dances in the air,
Wrapped in warmth, we share a glance,
In simple pleasures, hearts laid bare,
Together we weave a cherished romance.

Sunset hues paint the evening sky,
As we wander down familiar lanes,
Every memory like a soft sigh,
Echoing sweetly in our veins.

Holding onto these fragments of bliss,
In each heartbeat, we find our way,
Moments that savor, a gentle kiss,
Crafting our love in the light of day.

Whispers of the Heart

In the quiet of the night,
Soft murmurs draw us near.
Secrets linger in the dark,
As dreams ignite our fear.

With every gentle sigh,
Our souls begin to blend.
The echoes of our laughter,
A bond that will not end.

Beneath the moon's soft glow,
We share our deepest truths.
In whispers shared with love,
We find our endless youth.

Through trials we have faced,
Our hearts have learned to soar.
With every whispered promise,
We open every door.

Together we will journey,
Through valleys and through peaks.
With whispers of the heart,
It's love that truly speaks.

The Recipe of You and Me

A pinch of laughter, bright,
Two hearts that intertwine.
Stirred with passion's fire,
The taste of love divine.

Sauté dreams in the sun,
Let hope simmer with care.
Add a sprinkle of trust,
And joy is always there.

Mix in moments shared,
Knead with tender grace.
Bake in warmth and time,
In this cherished space.

Let flavors meld as one,
With each bite, we unite.
The recipe we made,
Brings comfort every night.

With every gentle stir,
Our hearts grow rich and free.
In the kitchen of our souls,
It's the recipe of you and me.

Ties that Blossom

Roots entwined beneath the ground,
Two hearts begin to grow.
Through seasons of our lives,
A bond that starts to show.

With every bloom of spring,
New colors fill the air.
The ties that bind us close,
Reveal the love we share.

In the warmth of summer's sun,
We dance beneath the trees.
Each laugh, a petal's fall,
Carried by the breeze.

As autumn leaves do sway,
We find our strength anew.
In the chill of winter's grasp,
Our hearts stay warm and true.

For as the years go by,
Our flowers bloom and thrive.
In every shade of love,
Together, we will strive.

Heartbeats in Harmony

In the rhythm of the night,
Two hearts create a song.
Beats aligned in unity,
Melodies that feel so strong.

With every pulse, a whisper,
Echoes soft and sweet.
The dance of us together,
Makes our world complete.

Through every rise and fall,
Our music flows like streams.
In heartbeats' gentle tune,
We weave our endless dreams.

In the chorus of the stars,
We find our place above.
Each note a step we take,
In the symphony of love.

Together we will sing,
In harmony so fine.
With heartbeats intertwined,
Your love forever mine.

The Embrace of Time

In twilight's glow, the shadows play,
Moments drift, then fade away.
Whispers of dreams on a silent breeze,
Time's gentle hands bring us to our knees.

Seasons change, yet hearts remain,
Weaving stories in joy and pain.
Each tick a heartbeat, each tock a sigh,
In the vastness of now, we learn to fly.

Memories linger like stars at night,
Guiding lost souls towards the light.
In the embrace of minutes, we find our place,
Lost in the beauty of time's warm grace.

Life's canvas painted with laughter and tears,
A tapestry woven with hopes and fears.
In the arms of eternity, we learn to roam,
For every heartbeat brings us back home.

Serene Conversations

Under the shade of an ancient tree,
Voices blend in harmony.
Gentle laughter, like a soft refrain,
In moments shared, we find our gain.

Eyes that meet, like rivers flow,
With every word, a bond will grow.
Silence speaks where words may fail,
In the stillness, our spirits sail.

Beneath the stars, our secrets unfold,
Echoes of dreams in stories told.
With every whisper, our souls align,
In serene conversations, we intertwine.

Time stands still in this quiet place,
Where thoughts dance softly, a tender grace.
In the warmth of trust, our fears depart,
For every exchange, a piece of the heart.

Soulful Reflections

In quiet corners of a restless mind,
We seek the truths that we hope to find.
Mirrors of life, they echo deep,
In the shadows, our secrets keep.

Whispers of wisdom float on air,
Beneath the surface, a silent prayer.
With every pause, we hear the call,
In soulful reflections, we rise or fall.

Holding moments like fragile glass,
Learning to cherish, letting time pass.
In the depths of silence, there's so much sound,
Where the answers lie, yet to be found.

From the canvas of night, stars will glean,
Reflecting the stories we've yet to mean.
In the heart's quiet chamber, we see our way,
Through soulful reflections at the close of day.

The Bridge of Belonging

In the distance stands a bridge so wide,
Uniting hearts on either side.
Step by step, a journey begins,
With open arms, the love pours in.

Voices blend in a chorus of cheer,
Across the expanse, we draw near.
Each footfall echoes a story shared,
In this sacred space, we feel prepared.

Together we build, each stone a gem,
A testament to where we've been.
Through storms and sunlight, we persevere,
On the bridge of belonging, we find our sphere.

With laughter and tears, we intertwine,
In the glow of belonging, our lives align.
No longer alone, we stand as one,
For in this embrace, our hearts have won.

Paths Intertwined

In the forest where shadows play,
Two wanderers find their way.
With laughter that dances in the air,
They share their dreams, a moment rare.

Each step they take a bond is formed,
Through whispers of leaves, their hearts warmed.
In the twilight, they pause and see,
The beauty of what it means to be.

As stars emerge in the dusky sky,
They recognize the reasons why.
Their journeys blend, as fate prescribes,
Together they walk, hearts as their guides.

Paths that cross were meant to twine,
In the dance of fate, a design divine.
And as the night wraps them in its glow,
They know true friendship is what they sow.

The Warmth of Kindred Spirits

In a quiet room filled with light,
Two souls connect, a heartwarming sight.
With stories shared and laughter bright,
Each moment glows, dispelling the night.

Tea cups clink, as tales unfold,
Of journeys taken, of dreams retold.
Their spirits dance in a gentle sway,
A bond formed strong, come what may.

With every smile, the warmth grows near,
In solace found, there's nothing to fear.
Through trials faced and joys embraced,
Their hearts entwined in time and space.

In the tapestry of life they weave,
Kindred spirits, who dare believe.
With every hug, the world seems wide,
In the warmth of friendship, they confide.

A Mosaic of Memories

Fragments of life in colors bright,
Pieces of laughter, shadows of light.
Each memory a tile, placed with care,
Creating a mosaic, a love laid bare.

In the corners, the whispers sing,
Of moments shared, the joy they bring.
The laughter echoes, the tears subside,
In this artwork, our hearts reside.

With every glance, a story unfolds,
In a gallery where time beholds.
Moments treasured, both sweet and sage,
Captured forever on life's vast page.

As seasons change, the colors shift,
Yet the essence remains, a timeless gift.
In this mosaic, our lives align,
Each memory a blessing, forever divine.

Canvas of Connection

On a canvas wide, colors collide,
With strokes of laughter, side by side.
Each hue a heartbeat, each line a tale,
Together we paint, in sunshine and gale.

Through the splashes of joy, the drips of pain,
We find our footing on life's refrain.
As brushes intertwine, our spirits blend,
Creating a masterpiece that seeks to mend.

In the gallery of hearts, we display,
The moments that formed us along the way.
A dance of emotions, a visual song,
On this canvas of connection, we belong.

With every layer, our stories grow,
A vibrant tapestry that we bestow.
In the essence of colors that brightly shine,
We find our truth, forever entwined.

The Comfort of Hearts

In stillness, hearts do beat,
A sanctuary, soft and sweet.
Wrapped in warmth of quiet sighs,
Trust unfolds beneath the skies.

Laughter dances, shadows play,
In gentle light, we find our way.
With whispered words, the night unfolds,
A tapestry of stories told.

Together we face each dawn,
In every moment, love is drawn.
Side by side, through joy and pain,
In each heart, we find our gain.

The comfort found in each embrace,
Transforms the world, a sacred space.
In every heartbeat, life extends,
A rhythm shared, where love transcends.

Silent glances, knowing smiles,
We journey far, across the miles.
In this bond, we truly thrive,
Together, we feel so alive.

The Rhythm of Connection

In every beat, a chord resounds,
Two souls entwined, love abounds.
The dance of fate, a song we share,
In every glance, a silent prayer.

Moments fleeting, yet they stay,
Whispered truths, lighting the way.
Hands held tight, a guiding force,
In this rhythm, we find our course.

Life's melody, soft and sweet,
In harmony, our hearts repeat.
With every laugh, every tear,
The music plays when you are near.

Time may shift, but we remain,
Through storms and sun, through joy and pain.
In every heartbeat, the song's alive,
Together, forever, we will thrive.

The rhythm guides us, steady, true,
In every moment, just me and you.
Through the verses, our story flows,
In this dance of love, it always grows.

Soulmates Under the Sky

Beneath the stars, our dreams align,
In whispered wishes, hearts entwine.
Two souls adrift, now anchored tight,
In moonlit glow, we find our light.

With every glance, a spark ignites,
In shared laughter, our spirit flights.
Through cosmic paths, we journey free,
In every moment, you and me.

The universe hums a tune so sweet,
Wherever we wander, love's heartbeat.
Hand in hand, we chase the dawn,
In this connection, we are reborn.

The heavens bear witness to our song,
Where we belong, where hearts are strong.
In the tapestry of life we weave,
With every breath, we believe.

Soulmates bound by fate's kind thread,
In this vast world, love's path we tread.
Together forever, under the sky,
In love's embrace, we learn to fly.

The Palette of Life Together

With vibrant hues, our days unfold,
In shades of laughter, dreams retold.
Each moment's brushstroke, rich and bold,
Together painting stories gold.

Strokes of joy, splashes of pain,
In every hue, love will remain.
A canvas bright with colors true,
In life's gallery, me and you.

With every sunset, hues collide,
Our masterpiece, we wear with pride.
In shadows cast, we find the light,
Creating beauty in the night.

The palette swirls, forever bound,
In every heartbeat, love resounds.
In every tear, a spark ignites,
Guiding us through the darkest nights.

Together we paint, day by day,
With every color, we find our way.
In every moment, joy and strife,
Together we craft the art of life.

Hearts in Sync

In quiet whispers, our souls collide,
A rhythm found in the evening tide.
With every glance, a story's told,
Two hearts in sync, they're brave and bold.

Underneath the starlit skies,
We share our dreams, we share our sighs.
The pulse of love, a gentle beat,
In harmony, our lives complete.

Through every storm, we stand as one,
Chasing shadows, we've just begun.
With laughter bright and tears that shine,
Together on this path divine.

In secret moments, hands entwine,
A silent vow that feels like rhyme.
With every joy and every pain,
Our hearts in sync, we will remain.

As seasons shift, and time runs fast,
We cherish moments, hold them fast.
A symphony of souls unique,
In perfect harmony, we speak.

The Unspoken Bond

In quiet corners, we find our way,
Through the words that we don't say.
An understanding that goes so deep,
In every moment, the bond we keep.

With fleeting glances, a knowing smile,
We journey together, mile by mile.
No need for words to bridge the gap,
In silence, we form our own map.

Through trials faced and joy embraced,
In shared glances, our fears are chased.
With laughter ringing clear and bright,
Our unspoken bond, a guiding light.

In the stillness, we hear the call,
A gentle nudge that binds us all.
With hearts that speak, we take a stand,
Forever linked, hand in hand.

In every heartbeat, in every sigh,
The unspoken bond will never die.
A treasure held, both rare and grand,
In quietude, we understand.

Cradled in Comfort

In evening's glow, where shadows play,
I find my solace at the end of day.
With gentle hands, the world unwinds,
Cradled in comfort, our hearts aligned.

With every sigh, the worries fade,
In your embrace, my fears are laid.
The softest touch can heal the soul,
Together we make each other whole.

Beneath the stars, in whispered tones,
We share our dreams, and love has grown.
With every laugh, the world feels right,
Cradled in comfort, we ignite.

In the tender moments, time stands still,
Each heartbeat echoes, love's sweet thrill.
With you beside me, all is clear,
Cradled in comfort, my heart you steer.

Through every storm, we hold the light,
In the darkest hours, you are my sight.
In love's warm embrace, we shall find,
A cradle of comfort, intertwined.

The Dance of Companions

In moonlit glow, two figures sway,
With silent steps, we find our way.
A dance of hearts, a gentle tune,
With every turn, we greet the moon.

Through laughter bright and whispers low,
In every movement, our spirits flow.
A pas de deux of trust and grace,
In this dance, we find our place.

With every dip, we share a dream,
A tapestry of light, a gleam.
In harmony, our souls unite,
The dance of companions, pure delight.

With each heartbeat, the rhythm stays,
Guiding our paths through life's array.
In this embrace, we lose the fight,
Together dancing into the night.

As music fades, we take a bow,
In memories woven, here and now.
The dance of companions, forever strong,
In this cherished melody, we belong.

Sips of Shared Joy

In a cup shared, laughter brews,
Sweet moments traded, nothing to lose.
Warmth flows like sunshine bright,
In every sip, pure delight.

Conversations dance, words like wine,
Crisp autumn evenings, all things align.
A toast to the bonds that softly grow,
With every sip, our hearts in tow.

Memories crafted, rich and bold,
Stories whispered, quietly told.
Friendships flourish with every embrace,
Each sip savored, a sacred space.

Together we rise, like morning's dew,
Connections deepened with every brew.
In this moment, time stands still,
With sips of joy, our hearts fulfill.

So raise your cup, let laughter flow,
In shared experiences, our spirits glow.
For in these sips, forever we find,
The joy of togetherness, intertwined.

The Light in Dark Places

In shadows thick, a glow appears,
Guiding us through our deepest fears.
A flicker bright, igniting our way,
Leading our hearts to a brand new day.

Hope's ember warms the chilling night,
Filling our souls with soft, sweet light.
Through trials faced and burdens shared,
Together we navigate, unprepared.

Serenity blooms where darkness loomed,
In the quiet moments, our strength resumed.
A beacon shines, piercing the gloom,
In each heartbeat, we find our room.

Hand in hand, we forge ahead,
With whispers of courage, softly said.
In the night's embrace, we learn to trust,
For in each other, we find what's just.

Let love illuminate the paths we tread,
Filling our lives with bright threads spread.
Through trials and triumphs, a light will guide,
In darkened places, we'll stand side by side.

Threads of Unbreakable Trust

Woven together, hearts entwined,
In every moment, our souls aligned.
A tapestry rich with laughter and tears,
Threads of trust bind us through the years.

In silence shared, our spirits soar,
In whispered vows, we promise more.
Each secret held, like a precious gem,
With threads so strong, we'll never stem.

Through storms we weather, side by side,
With every challenge, love is our guide.
An unbreakable bond, steadfast and true,
With threads of trust that only grew.

In shadows cast by doubts and fears,
We find our light, through laughter and cheers.
Together we rise, no matter the gust,
For in our hearts, lives unbreakable trust.

Let time unfurl our journey grand,
With each step taken, hand in hand.
In every stitch of this life we weave,
Our threads of trust are what we believe.

Seasons of Togetherness

As springtime flowers begin to bloom,
We gather close, dispelling the gloom.
In sunlit days, we laugh and play,
In nature's arms, we find our way.

Summer nights, warm breezes abate,
Shared whispers linger, never too late.
Together we bask, as stars ignite,
In the tapestry of love, pure and bright.

Autumn leaves fall, a gentle sigh,
With fireside chats, as days slip by.
In every hue, our spirits merge,
Through seasons shifting, we feel the surge.

Winter's chill may frost the ground,
Yet in each heart, our warmth is found.
Snuggled close, through storms we tread,
Together we stand, where love is bred.

In every season, our story told,
In moments cherished, memories unfold.
For in this journey, hand in hand,
The gift of togetherness, forever we stand.

Embracing Shared Light

In the soft dawn, we arise,
Beneath the canvas of the skies.
Hearts as one in radiant bloom,
Illuminating every room.

Together we weave our dreams,
With laughter like sunlight beams.
Hand in hand, we find our way,
Through the light of each new day.

Whispers float on gentle air,
Promises made, a bond so rare.
In our eyes, a spark shines bright,
Embracing all shared light.

As shadows fade, love takes flight,
Guiding souls through the night.
In this journey, we ignite,
A flame that grows, a warm delight.

With every step, a song unfolds,
In harmony, our stories told.
Together, we light the night,
In the glow of shared delight.

Whispers of Togetherness

In the hush of twilight's tale,
Whispers of love paint the vale.
With every glance, a secret shared,
In the silence, hearts are bared.

Fingers brushed like summer breeze,
In these moments, time can freeze.
Every breath, a tender sigh,
Two souls dancing 'neath the sky.

Starlit paths lead us afar,
Guided softly by our star.
Tangled in dreams, we find our place,
Wrapped in warmth, a loving grace.

Laughter mingles with the night,
In these whispers, all feels right.
Together, we laugh, we sing,
Celebrating what love can bring.

As the moon casts silver light,
We hold each other, hearts so bright.
In this sacred space, we know,
Togetherness helps love grow.

The Tapestry of Us

Threads of laughter and of tears,
Woven tightly through the years.
Every color tells a tale,
The fabric knit, we shall not fail.

In the loom of life, we stand,
Weaving dreams with our own hands.
Every stitch, a memory spun,
In the tapestry, we've begun.

Softly whispered hopes align,
Creating patterns, yours and mine.
In the shadows, light will play,
Guiding us along the way.

Through the storms and sunny days,
Unity in countless ways.
In the rich texture of our bond,
A legacy that lingers fond.

Threads of gold and threads of blue,
All collected, me and you.
In this tapestry, we trust,
A work of art, a must.

Laughter Underneath Stars

In the night with stars aglow,
We gather close, letting joy flow.
Laughter dances on the breeze,
A symphony that puts us at ease.

Underneath the cosmic dome,
We find in each other a home.
Stories shared, our spirits soar,
In this moment, we want for more.

With every chuckle, worries fade,
In the warmth of laughter, we're remade.
Together we shape the night,
Every glance, a shared delight.

Stars twinkle, the world feels right,
Kindred souls in the soft moonlight.
With echoes of laughter bright,
We embrace this perfect night.

So here we are, just you and me,
In laughter's grasp, we're truly free.
Underneath the stars, we trust,
In this moment, love is a must.

A Floral Pathway

Petals fall like whispers, soft,
Beneath the sun's warm glow.
Colors dance in gentle breeze,
As fragrant dreams arise below.

Winding trails of vibrant hue,
Guide the heart to wander free.
Each bloom tells a tale anew,
Of hope, and love's sweet memory.

Buds awaken with the dawn,
While shadows stretch and play.
Every step brings life along,
On this floral pathway's way.

Dew-kissed leaves in morning's light,
Reflect the journey's grace.
Nature weaves its pure delight,
In every cherished space.

In the garden's quiet peace,
Time stands still, a tender pause.
Amidst the blooms, hearts find release,
In the beauty of nature's cause.

Echoing Laughter

In distant fields, joy resounds,
Laughter dances on the air.
Bubbles of delight abound,
In moments bright, we share.

Children's giggles, pure and free,
Bouncing like the summer breeze.
Echoes blend in harmony,
A symphony of playful tease.

In cozy rooms where stories flow,
Laughter paints the walls with cheer.
Each chuckle adds a vibrant glow,
A melody for all to hear.

Friendship blooms in laughter's light,
Binding hearts in joyful glee.
Every joke a spark, a kite,
Soaring high, wild and free.

As twilight falls with gentle sighs,
Echoes linger, sweet and clear.
In laughter's warmth, our spirit flies,
Together, love, and joy appears.

The Palette of Togetherness

With every hue, our stories blend,
Brush strokes of both joy and pain.
In canvas bright, our colors mend,
Creating life with love's refrain.

We splash our dreams in vibrant ways,
A tapestry of shared embrace.
In timeless dance, our spirits sway,
Together, we find our rightful place.

The shades of hope and laughter bright,
Each line defines our bond so true.
In darkness too, we find our light,
A palette forged with every hue.

With brushes dipped in trust and care,
We paint a world, both bold and new.
In every stroke, our hearts laid bare,
Together, weaving dreams pursue.

So let us create, hand in hand,
A masterpiece of love's design.
In this grand art, forever stand,
The palette of our hearts align.

Rays of Empathy

In sunlight's glow, we find our way,
Through shadows that in silence creep.
Each heartbeat speaks, a soft array,
Of kindness sown in hearts we keep.

A gentle touch, a knowing glance,
Connects our souls in shared embrace.
With every act, we weave a dance,
Of understanding, warmth, and grace.

The world becomes a brighter place,
When empathy begins to flow.
In every smile, in every trace,
The love we share begins to grow.

No storm can break our woven ties,
As we uplift each other's dreams.
In unity, our spirits rise,
Creating light in life's extremes.

So let us shine like morning rays,
With kindness as our guiding light.
In every word, in myriad ways,
Empathy can chase the night.

Treasures Unearthed

In the depths of earth below,
Hidden gems await to glow.
Whispers of the past, we find,
Secrets kept in nature's mind.

Every stone, a story told,
Of journeys brave, both young and old.
As we dig beneath the skin,
We discover worlds within.

From silence, jewels come alive,
In forgotten places, dreams survive.
Nature's bounty, rich and rare,
In the soil, hope's treasure fair.

Hands in dirt, we greet the day,
With every find, our hearts will sway.
The past and present intertwine,
In unearthing, we define.

With each layer, lessons grow,
In the dark, we learn to sow.
Together, we embrace the quest,
Finding solace in the rest.

The Cradle of Shared Dreams

In the hush of twilight's glow,
Together, seeds of wishes sow.
Each heart a lantern, fierce and bright,
Guiding us through the darkest night.

Voices blend, a sweet embrace,
In this shared and sacred space.
Dreams awaken, hopes take flight,
Cradled gently, our spirits light.

Hand in hand, we walk the line,
With every step, our hearts align.
In laughter's warmth, we find our way,
As dreams weave through the night and day.

Stories shared like woven threads,
In tapestry where love spreads.
In every heartbeat, echoes play,
The cradle rocks our fears away.

Together strong, we rise anew,
With every dream, we chase the blue.
In the cradle, we are whole,
United in the dance of soul.

Warmth of Shared Journeys

Through winding roads, we laugh and tread,
In stories shared, our worries shed.
The warmth between us ever glows,
In the light of friendship, love grows.

With open hearts, we dare to roam,
Creating paths that lead us home.
Every step, a memory made,
In shared journeys, fears will fade.

Through valleys low and mountains high,
We lift each other, we reach the sky.
With hands entwined, we make our place,
In every sunset, we find grace.

In whispers soft, our secrets bloom,
In pastures wide, we shed our gloom.
With every mile, we write our tale,
In the warmth of love, we prevail.

Together strong, we face the dawn,
In shared journeys, we have drawn
A canvas bright with colors bold,
In the warmth of dreams retold.

Rainbows of Trust

In stormy skies, we find the light,
Through clouds of doubt, our bonds ignite.
Each raindrop falls, a promise clear,
In rainbows bright, we hold each dear.

Colors blend in tender grace,
Trust a bridge, no time can erase.
Through trials faced, our spirits rise,
In unity, our strength defies.

With every hue, our hearts unfold,
Painting stories waiting told.
In laughter's echo, joy ascends,
In trust, we find the finest friends.

We walk the line, our hands entwined,
In every trust, new paths we find.
With open hearts, we see the view,
In rainbows bright, our dreams come true.

Together we embrace the storm,
In vibrant arcs, we feel the warmth.
Through the rain, our spirits soar,
In rainbows of trust, we want for more.

Roots of Togetherness

In the quiet earth we grow,
Entwined beneath the surface,
Connected by the love we show,
A tapestry of shared purpose.

Every storm that shakes the ground,
Strengthens our steadfast embrace,
In this bond, we are unbound,
Love's resilience finds its place.

Through the seasons we will thrive,
Nurtured by our hopes and dreams,
In this union, we alive,
Together, stronger than we seem.

Roots that reach where hearts can touch,
Anchored deep in trust and care,
Through the trials, we love much,
In harmony, our spirits share.

Together, in this sacred space,
United by our journeys' start,
In every challenge we embrace,
The roots of us will never part.

Bonds Beneath the Surface

Whispers dance in twilight's glow,
Secrets shared in silent sighs,
Like rivers deep, our feelings flow,
Beneath the world, the truth lies.

In shadows cast by doubts and fears,
We lift each other, hand in hand,
Supporting dreams through all the years,
Together, we will always stand.

A tapestry of life we weave,
With threads of laughter, love, and tears,
In every moment, we believe,
Our bond will carry through the years.

Roots entwined through thick and thin,
From darkest soil, our flowers bloom,
In the warmth of love, we begin,
Together banishing the gloom.

Through undiscovered depths we swim,
Our hearts beat strong beneath the waves,
In the abyss, our light won't dim,
For these bonds are what love saves.

The Garden of Our Souls

In the garden where dreams reside,
Petals whisper secrets sweet,
Blooming brightly side by side,
In this place, our hearts will meet.

Each seed we plant, a story sown,
Tender roots intertwine and grow,
Nurtured by the love we've known,
Our vibrant colors start to show.

Through the changing seasons, we endure,
Weathering the storms that come our way,
With hands together, hearts so sure,
We cultivate a brand new day.

Among the flowers, we will roam,
Finding solace in our embrace,
In this garden, we have grown,
Together, we've created space.

With every bloom, our dreams take flight,
A testament to all we share,
In the garden, hearts burn bright,
For love's the seed we chose to care.

Strong Like the Willow

Bending low, yet standing tall,
The willow sways with gentle grace,
In the wind, it hears the call,
A dance of strength in every place.

Through the storms that rage and howl,
It finds its footing, deep and sure,
With roots that dig, it won't just prowl,
In resilience, it will endure.

Like the willow, we will bend,
Adapting to the tides of life,
With every twist, our spirits mend,
In love's embrace, we'll face the strife.

Whispered promises in the breeze,
Carried softly through the night,
With each moment, heart's unease,
Turns to strength, transforming light.

So let us stand, like willow trees,
With branches stretching towards the sky,
In unity, we'll find our ease,
Strong together, never shy.

Melodies of Affection

In whispers soft, the night conveys,
A tune of love that gently sways.
Beneath the stars, our hearts align,
In every note, your hand in mine.

Through fleeting moments, sweet and bright,
We dance in shadows, lost in light.
With every laugh, with every sigh,
Our souls entwined, we learn to fly.

In every heartbeat, music plays,
A symphony of endless days.
Together we compose our song,
In melodies where we belong.

The echoes linger, soft and sweet,
Each harmony feels so complete.
In tender notes, forever found,
Love's gentle whispers all around.

Heartstrings of Joy

With every smile, a spark ignites,
Connection blooms like morning lights.
In laughter shared, our spirits rise,
We find our hopes in open skies.

Through every challenge, hand in hand,
Together we will bravely stand.
In every tear, a story grows,
The heartstrings pull, and joy just flows.

In simple moments, bliss we find,
The warmth of you, forever kind.
Each heartbeat sings a tune so rare,
With love expressed in every flare.

In tender glances, sparks will fly,
Connection that can never die.
Through endless days and peaceful nights,
Our joy, a dance of purest lights.

A Soft Landing

As feathers drift on gentle winds,
I find my peace, where love begins.
In open arms, a safe embrace,
With every touch, a sacred space.

The world outside can fade away,
In this cocoon, forever stay.
Through storms that rage and skies that frown,
We build our dreams on solid ground.

With whispered thoughts, the softest words,
In silence shared, our hearts can soar.
Together we explore the skies,
In every glance, our spirits rise.

Through every step, a quiet grace,
A journey taken, face to face.
In love's sweet arms, we always land,
A tender path, forever planned.

Umbrellas of Care

In rain's soft fall, a shelter found,
With open arms, we circle 'round.
Through storms of life, together stand,
With umbrellas bright, we'll face the land.

When shadows loom and fears arise,
Together, we will brave the skies.
With every drop, our bond will grow,
A steady love that steals the show.

In laughter shared through chilly air,
We find our warmth in moments rare.
With every challenge, we take flight,
An anchored heart through darkest night.

In tender gestures, kindness shared,
Life's fleeting trials, all prepared.
With love as bold as colors flare,
We walk united, free of care.

Embrace of the Heart

In the warmth of a gentle night,
Two souls find their way to light.
Whispers soft like a tender breeze,
Held together with subtle ease.

Every glance a silent vow,
Time stands still, illuminated now.
In the depth of shared embrace,
Each heartbeat finds its rightful place.

Laughter echoes, shadows dance,
In this moment, the perfect chance.
With every word, a melody,
Together crafting harmony.

Through storms and trials, they will stand,
Hand in hand, a united band.
In the hush of dawn's first light,
Hope awakens, shining bright.

The world fades in the distance,
Here, there's only pure existence.
In the embrace of heart's domain,
Love's true essence shall remain.

Threads of Harmony

In the tapestry of life we weave,
Each thread a story, you believe.
Colors blend in perfect grace,
Creating patterns in time and space.

An embrace of different hues,
Bringing forth the love we choose.
In every stitch, a shared dream,
Together, we are a flowing stream.

Like notes in a symphony played,
In unity, our fears are laid.
Stronger together, we rise and fall,
Finding solace when shadows call.

In laughter shared and tears that fall,
We discover the strength in it all.
A circle unbroken, vibrant and true,
In this dance, it begins with you.

With every journey, new threads spun,
Creating a bond that can't be undone.
Through the chaos, we find our way,
In the tapestry of life, we stay.

Serenity in Silence

In the stillness of the night,
Peace whispers soft and light.
Stars twinkle in endless skies,
Beneath them, true serenity lies.

With every breath, the world slows down,
In quiet moments, wear no crown.
Nature sings a soothing tune,
Underneath the watchful moon.

In solitude, our thoughts unwind,
Beauty in silence, intertwined.
A gentle heart, a listening ear,
In stillness found, doubts disappear.

Each heartbeat a soft refrain,
Embracing calm, releasing pain.
Finding strength within the pause,
In the quiet, a world of cause.

As dawn approaches, colors bloom,
In silence, we dispel the gloom.
Cherished moments, pure and bright,
In serenity, we find our light.

The Dance of Companionship

In the glow of twilight's grace,
Two hearts join in a slow embrace.
With every step, they navigate,
The rhythm of love, their shared fate.

Through laughter and challenges faced,
Together they learn, they've embraced.
A partnership that blooms and grows,
In this dance, true love bestows.

In every twirl, a story told,
Memories woven, strong and bold.
Through the storms that life can bring,
Their hearts remain forever spring.

With gentle turns and swift declines,
They find their way through tangled lines.
In harmony, their spirits soar,
In each other's arms, they explore.

Though steps may falter, they remain,
In this dance, a sweet refrain.
Together forever, hand in hand,
In the dance of companionship, they stand.

Resonance of the Heartstrings

In twilight's soft embrace, we find,
Whispers of love, entwined and kind.
A melody dances, sweet and clear,
Echoes of laughter, drawing near.

Threads of connection, bold and bright,
A symphony woven through day and night.
Each heartbeat strums a gentle tune,
Drawing us closer, like stars to the moon.

In moments fleeting, we discover gold,
The stories of hearts, in silence told.
Hands intertwine, souls reach for more,
A resonance shared, at love's open door.

Through trials faced and storms we brave,
The music in us, forever to wave.
In melodies crafted by fate's own hand,
We journey together, a united band.

So let the strings of our hearts play true,
In every whisper, in all we pursue.
For in this dance, we rise and shine,
Resonance of heartstrings, yours and mine.

Embracing the Ordinary

Morning light spills on the kitchen floor,
A simple cup, familiar lore.
In gentle rhythms, life unfolds,
Beauty found in stories told.

Stooped down low by autumn's grace,
Fallen leaves in a soft embrace.
Each mundane task, a sacred art,
In quiet moments, we find our heart.

Laughter echoes through the halls,
Children's footsteps, love's sweet calls.
The everyday shines with quiet pride,
In the ordinary, our dreams reside.

With each sunset painting the sky,
We learn to dance, to laugh, to cry.
Finding joy in each fleeting breath,
In simple things, we conquer death.

So let us cherish what appears small,
In the routine, we hear the call.
For in these moments, life's true goal,
Is to embrace the beauty of the whole.

Bonds Beyond Time

In shadows deep, a memory lies,
Whispering secrets beneath the skies.
Across the ages, love's gentle touch,
Binds our souls, it means so much.

Threads of time weave a tapestry,
Colors of laughter, you and me.
Moments shared, though far apart,
Eternal echoes, a sacred heart.

In quiet gazes, we see the past,
Bonds of spirit, built to last.
When time stands still, our hearts align,
A testament to love divine.

From one lifetime to the next we stray,
In every heartbeat, we find our way.
Connections formed that cannot fade,
In the labyrinth where memories wade.

So let us cherish this timeless grace,
The threads of love we still embrace.
For in each lifetime, near or far,
Bonds beyond time, we are who we are.

The Garden of Hearts

In the garden where dreams take flight,
Petals unfurl in morning light.
Each bloom a whisper, soft and true,
Tales of love, fresh as the dew.

With every color, a story to tell,
In the heart's deep soil, we all dwell.
Roots intertwined, we grow as one,
Nurtured by warmth of the setting sun.

Bees buzz softly, a gentle tune,
Fragrance fills the air, sweet as noon.
In this haven where moments dwell,
Every heartbeat, a secret spell.

Through changing seasons, we'll endure,
In the garden, we plant and secure.
Harvesting laughter, friendship's embrace,
In love's bountiful, sacred space.

So let the blooms of our hearts unfold,
In the sunlight's reach, be brave and bold.
For in this garden, truths impart,
A timeless dance, the garden of hearts.

Landmarks of Laughter

In the park where giggles play,
Children chase the clouds away.
Laughter echoes, bright and clear,
Moments frozen, held so dear.

Jokes exchanged beneath the trees,
Heartfelt smiles in every breeze.
A playground buzzes, joy ignites,
Innocence, pure, takes its flights.

Friends gather, stories intertwine,
Each tale woven, rich like wine.
Memories crafted, laughter's art,
A gentle balm for every heart.

From sunlit days to starlit nights,
We paint our world with joyful sights.
In every chuckle, bonds grow tight,
A tapestry of pure delight.

In every landmark, laughter stands,
Creating joy with loving hands.
Forever cherished, these traces stay,
Guiding us along our way.

The Bloom of Loyalty

In gardens where friendships bloom,
Roots entwined, dispel the gloom.
Each petal whispers soft and true,
A bond unbroken, me and you.

Through storms we stand, a sturdy tree,
Shelter found in unity.
With every trial that we face,
Loyal hearts, a warm embrace.

Seasons change but we remain,
Sowing trust, reaping the grain.
In laughter's shade or sorrow's rain,
Together always, joy and pain.

Hand in hand, we forge ahead,
In the bloom of loyalty spread.
A tapestry of memories spun,
In every beat, our hearts are one.

From early dawn to twilight's end,
We are the echo, we are the blend.
Through every challenge, side by side,
In loyal faith, we take our stride.

Reflections in Harmony

On tranquil lakes where ripples weave,
Reflections dance, we dare believe.
Each moment shared, a melody,
In perfect tune, just you and me.

Voices blend like birds in flight,
Creating waves that feel so right.
With every note, our spirits soar,
In harmony, we seek for more.

Gentle breezes carry our songs,
Uniting hearts that have been strong.
In quiet corners, laughter gleams,
Reflections of our shared dreams.

Through changing times, our bond stays true,
In every chord, I find you too.
Together weaving, joy and grace,
In life's sweet tune, we find our place.

With open arms, we face the dawn,
In every sound, new paths are drawn.
The music swells, and love is found,
Reflections in harmony surround.

The Soundtrack of Togetherness

In every laugh, a note is played,
The soundtrack of our memories laid.
Melodies of joy intertwine,
In the symphony that's yours and mine.

From quiet whispers to joyous screams,
Life's vibrant rhythm fuels our dreams.
Together we dance, hearts in sync,
In every moment, our spirits link.

Familiar songs fill the air,
A binding force, a timeless flare.
With every beat, we move as one,
A duet shining like the sun.

Through highs and lows, the notes remain,
Crafting beauty amid the pain.
Each tear and smile, a precious chord,
Creating harmony, our rich reward.

So let the music play on strong,
In every heart, we all belong.
In the soundtrack of togetherness,
Love's sweet refrain, we shall profess.

A Quilt of Care

Stitch by stitch, our stories weave,
Threads of warmth, in hearts believe.
Colors bright, in every seam,
A cozy place, to dream and dream.

Each patch a tale, of joy or pain,
Embracing love, like gentle rain.
Wrapped in comfort, fears take flight,
In this embrace, all feels right.

Through seasons change, the quilt will hold,
Memories cherished, stories told.
In every fold, a whisper glows,
A testament, to love that grows.

When night descends, and shadows play,
The quilt will keep the chill at bay.
With every stitch, we nurture care,
A tapestry of bonds we share.

In quiet moments, we find our peace,
As threads entwine, and worries cease.
A quilt of care, forever near,
A soft reminder, love is here.

Maps of Memory

Beneath the stars, our journeys start,
Each path a marker, etching art.
With every turn, new tales unfold,
In maps of memory, life is told.

Footprints linger on the sand,
With laughter echoing, hand in hand.
Moments captured in time's embrace,
Each memory, a sacred place.

Through forests deep and mountains high,
We wandered wide, beneath the sky.
The ink of joy, drawn in the air,
With every breath, we felt the care.

Layers of time, like whispered dreams,
In maps of memory, endless streams.
We chart our course, through joy and strife,
Each line a thread, connecting life.

As seasons pass and ages blend,
In every map, our hearts descend.
For in the end, what truly lasts,
Are maps of memory, from our past.

Hearthstone of Affection

In the hearth's glow, we gather 'round,
With warmth and laughter, love is found.
Fires crackle, stories blend,
In this haven, hearts mend.

A cup of tea, shared with care,
The fragrance of home fills the air.
Every glance, a gentle sign,
In this space, our souls align.

Through the years, the embers spark,
Guiding us through the dark.
With every hug, a promise made,
In the hearthstone's glow, fears fade.

Traditions cherished, bonds grown tight,
In this circle, everything feels right.
With every meal, a story shared,
Love's foundation, always bared.

As nights grow long and seasons wane,
In the hearthstone's warmth, we remain.
A sanctuary, forever our place,
In the glow of love, we find our grace.

Whirlwind of Shared Adventures

With laughter bright, we take our flight,
In a whirlwind of joy, day turns to night.
Through valleys deep and mountains tall,
Together we rise, together we fall.

Every journey, a story to tell,
In the heart of friendship, we dwell.
With every adventure, our spirits soar,
In shared moments, we find much more.

From city streets to oceans wide,
As partners in crime, we take the ride.
The world unfolds, with wonders vast,
In the whirlwind, we hold fast.

With each new step, new dreams in sight,
Chasing the dawn, embracing the light.
In every heartbeat, the thrill of chase,
In this whirlwind, we find our place.

Together we'll seek, together we'll see,
In the dance of life, just you and me.
A whirlwind of shared adventures, our song,
In the tapestry of life, where we belong.

A Symphony of Souls

In the quiet night we sing,
Notes of love in gentle sway.
Hearts entwined, a vibrant ring,
Together, we find our way.

Each whisper carries a tune,
Caressing dreams in soft embrace.
Underneath the watchful moon,
We dance to time's timeless grace.

Echoes of laughter will last,
Melodies of joy arise.
In this moment, no future past,
We are stars in boundless skies.

Chords of kindness fill the air,
Harmony of souls aligned.
Through the trials, we will care,
In each other, truth we find.

So let the symphony play on,
In every note, we are whole.
With every dusk, a new dawn,
In unity, we are soul.

Glimmers of Affection

In the shadows, soft lights glow,
Tender gestures, sweet and slight.
In glances shared, feelings flow,
Affection blooms, pure and bright.

With every smile that we share,
Courage grows, fears dissipate.
In a moment, hearts laid bare,
Time slows down, love navigates.

Echoes of laughter weave tight,
A tapestry of warm embrace.
In the dark, you are my light,
Every heartbeat, love's pure grace.

Though storms may rage and winds howl,
We find shelter, hand in hand.
In quiet moments, hear the growl,
Of love's promise, we will stand.

These glimmers, they never fade,
In every story that we tell.
Through the memories we've made,
In each other, we find our spell.

Lanterns in the Dark

Through the night, our lanterns shine,
Guiding paths with gentle grace.
In your eyes, warmth divine,
Comfort found in your embrace.

Every shadow hides a fear,
But your light will lead the way.
In your presence, doubts disappear,
Together, we chase gray away.

With each step, the world ignites,
Illuminated by our dreams.
In the silence, love incites,
Hope is more than what it seems.

Though darkness may try to creep,
We'll stand firm, our spirits strong.
With our lanterns, faith we keep,
In this dance, we both belong.

So here we are, hand in hand,
Lanterns bright against the night.
With every heartbeat, we will stand,
Together, we forge our light.

Seeds of Trust

In the soil of our shared dreams,
We plant the seeds of fate today.
Watered by love's gentle streams,
Our trust will grow in every way.

In time's embrace, strong roots will shoot,
Branching out, reaching for the sun.
With every choice, we bear the fruit,
Of a bond that can't be undone.

Through the seasons, we will tend,
Nurturing what we've come to know.
In the garden, trust won't end,
As we watch our love freely grow.

Even storms may come and go,
But our foundation will hold tight.
With every high and even low,
We cultivate our shared light.

So here we stand, side by side,
With the seeds of trust we've sown.
In this journey, hearts open wide,
Together, we have truly grown.

The Fire that Warms

In the hearth where embers glow,
We gather close, the world below.
Warmth radiates from soul to soul,
A flickering light that makes us whole.

Hearts entwined in gentle sway,
In silence, we find words to say.
The flames dance high, stories unfurl,
Binding us tight in this small world.

Through the smoke, we see the past,
Moments forged, their shadows cast.
Together we face the night so bold,
With each crackle, a memory told.

As twilight melts into the dawn,
The fire dims, yet love lives on.
Though embers fade, our bonds remain,
In the warmth of hearts, we've gained.

So let us stoke this sacred flame,
With every laugh, in joy, we claim.
For love is the fire that always warms,
Through life's tempests, it transforms.

Tides of Mutual Respect

Like waves that dance upon the shore,
We ebb and flow, forevermore.
In harmony, our spirits rise,
Beneath the vast and open skies.

With every push, we gently learn,
The tides return, for which we yearn.
Respect is rooted deep in trust,
In kindness, we find what is just.

A beacon bright, in darkest hours,
We share the weight, we share the flowers.
From differences, our strength is born,
In unity, each heart is worn.

Ripples spread from acts so small,
In every rise, we hear the call.
Together we face the storms that clash,
For in our bonds, we find our path.

And as the tides recede and swell,
In every heart, there lies a well.
Of mutual respect, we weave our fate,
Building bridges, never too late.

Mosaic of Laughter

In moments shared, our laughter bright,
Colors blend, taking flight.
Each chuckle, a piece of art,
A joyful song from every heart.

From silly jokes to joyous cries,
In every smile, love never lies.
Fragments of fun, they intertwine,
A tapestry of mirth divine.

We gather close, beneath the sun,
In every giggle, we have won.
The artwork forms, exquisite, rare,
A mosaic of moments, bright and fair.

Through treasured laughs, we heal the soul,
In every crack, a glimpse of whole.
With every layer, memories stay,
Laughter, the color of our play.

So let us weave this joyous thread,
In every tear, where joy is bred.
For laughter's gift is ours to keep,
A mosaic that makes our hearts leap.

Echoes of Heartfelt Words

In whispers soft, our truths emerge,
From deep within, where feelings surge.
Each word a note, a gentle plea,
Resonating through you and me.

In twilight's glow, our voices blend,
Rich melodies that never end.
With empathy, we turn the page,
Heartfelt echoes, wisdom's sage.

Compassion flows like rivers wide,
In every tale, we find our guide.
Through laughter, tears, we pave the way,
In echoes of words, we find our stay.

The stories shared, both old and new,
Connect us all, in skies so blue.
In every line, a bond is forged,
Through echoes of words, our hearts enlarged.

So let us speak, let voices rise,
In every heart, a hopeful sigh.
With every word, we bridge the space,
Through heartfelt echoes, love's embrace.

A Serenade of Friendship

In laughter's glow, our spirits soar,
Echoes of joy, we both explore.
Through every trial, hand in hand,
Together we bloom, like flowers in sand.

Moments cherished, memories made,
With every smile, our doubts do fade.
Trust like a bridge, strong and true,
In this bond, I find my view.

Whispers at dusk, secrets we share,
Nothing compares to friend, so rare.
In silence, we find our hearts align,
A melody sweet, forever entwined.

Paths may wander, miles apart,
Yet you remain, deep in my heart.
In every shadow, your light remains,
A serenade soft, through joys and pains.

So raise a glass, a toast to us,
In friendship's embrace, we place our trust.
For in this life, through thick and thin,
It's you, my friend, who helps me win.

Timeless Conversations

In the quiet dawn, we sit and talk,
Words dance like leaves on a winding walk.
Threads of wisdom weave through the air,
Every sentence crafted with tender care.

Sunsets bring stories, tales from the past,
Moments we treasure, too bright to last.
In every silence, meaning flows deep,
A bond so rich, it stirs me from sleep.

Life's winding road, we navigate bold,
Sharing our secrets, our hopes, and our gold.
With laughter and tears, like rivers they blend,
In timeless conversations, we find our mend.

Stars twinkle down as we dream and share,
Ideas unleashed, floating in air.
In the night's embrace, our voices unite,
Creating a tapestry, woven in light.

Through thick and thin, come what may,
Together we journey, never to sway.
In every exchange, my heart sings clear,
For moments with you are treasures I hold dear.

The Essence of Us

In every glance, a story unfolds,
In each gentle touch, a warmth that holds.
Whispers of love, painted in trust,
In the essence of us, forever robust.

Threads of connection, woven so tight,
In laughter and tears, we ignite the night.
Two souls entwined, a beautiful dance,
In the rhythm of life, we find our chance.

Seasons may change, and time may bend,
Yet our spirit will not break or end.
In quiet moments, in echoes of laughter,
We cherish the present, ever after.

With every heartbeat, a promise unfolds,
In the essence of us, true love never molds.
Through storms and rain, we find our glow,
With every shared moment, together we grow.

In the tapestry of life, our colors blend,
A vivid portrait, on you I depend.
In the essence of us, I see my way,
With you by my side, come what may.

Flames of Kindness

In a world so vast, let kindness ignite,
A spark of compassion, lighting the night.
With every gesture, warmth we create,
Flames of kindness that never abate.

Through simple acts, we change the game,
A smile in the dark, never the same.
With open hearts, we touch the divine,
In the flames of kindness, our spirits align.

Let kindness be the song that we sing,
A melody sweet, in each little thing.
From stranger to friend, we bridge the divide,
Together we stand, with love as our guide.

In the ashes of hate, let forgiveness arise,
A fire of grace, under tender skies.
With every flame, may we shine ever bright,
In the warmth of kindness, we find our light.

So gather around, let our hearts embrace,
In the glow of our love, there's always a place.
For in this madness, we learn to be free,
In the flames of kindness, find unity.

Nurtured by Laughter

In the garden of delight, we play,
Where joy dances bright, come what may.
Laughter like sunshine, warm and bright,
Nurtures our souls, igniting the light.

Friends gather close, hearts intertwined,
Sharing sweet stories, happiness unconfined.
In every chuckle, life's worries cease,
Moments of joy, the sweetest peace.

With every giggle, our spirits lift,
A precious bond, a treasured gift.
Together we weave through laughter's embrace,
Creating a world, a beautiful space.

Through trials and storms, we stand tall,
Supporting each other, answering the call.
In laughter, we find our truest way,
Nurtured by love, come what may.

So let us sing, let our voices ring,
In this chorus of laughter, our spirits take wing.
For in joy we discover, in play we grow,
Nurtured by laughter, forever we'll flow.

Blossoms in the Breeze

Petals unfurl beneath the sun,
Whispers of spring, a race begun.
Blossoms sway gently in the breeze,
Nature's soft music, a moment to seize.

Colors collide, vibrant and bright,
Painting the world in pure delight.
Each bloom tells a tale, a secret to share,
In the dance of the flowers, love fills the air.

Beneath the vast sky, horizons expand,
A tapestry woven by nature's hand.
Together we wander, through fields so free,
Amongst the blossoms, just you and me.

Time slows down as we walk side by side,
In the arm of the breeze, there's nothing to hide.
With laughter as petals, we float and we sway,
In this garden of dreams, forever we'll stay.

So let the blossoms show us the way,
In the heart of the moment, come what may.
With every soft breeze, a promise we feel,
Life's sweetest blooms, a love that is real.

Collective Joy

In unity we rise, hearts aglow,
Together we shine, together we grow.
A tapestry woven from dreams we share,
In the warmth of our bond, we find comfort there.

Every laugh echoed in vibrant delight,
Collective joy brightening the night.
With an open hand and a listening ear,
We build a small world where love conquers fear.

Through storms we weather, side by side,
In the circle of friends, we take pride.
Together we dance, in step with the beat,
In this symphony of life, our hearts repeat.

With every hug shared, a ripple of grace,
Filling the void of this vast, empty space.
The power of love ignites the flame,
In our collective joy, we're never the same.

So let's gather close, let our spirits soar,
In this joyful embrace, forever explore.
With laughter as glue, we'll conquer our strife,
In the bliss of our bond, we find the light of life.

Flickers of Support

In shadows we stand, hand in hand,
Flickers of support in a vast land.
Through valleys of doubt, we shine bright,
Together we gather, igniting the light.

Every whisper shared, a beacon of hope,
With kindness and care, we learn how to cope.
A glance of compassion, a smile to show,
In the journey of life, together we grow.

Through burdens we carry, we lighten the load,
With love as our compass, we'll find our road.
Each word a spark, igniting the fire,
In the heart of connection, we rise higher.

With simple gestures, we bridge the divide,
In the flickers of support, our souls collide.
For in every struggle, we find a way,
Together we navigate life's winding sway.

So lean on my shoulder, I'll be there too,
In the flickers of support, we'll see it through.
With hearts intertwined, we'll face each new day,
In love and connection, forever we'll stay.